Why You
Will Marry the
Wrong Person
&
Other Essays

Why You Will Marry the Wrong Person

The School of Life

Published in 2017 by The School of Life
First published in the USA in 2018
70 Marchmont Street, London WC1N 1AB
Copyright © The School of Life 2017
Designed and typeset by Marcia Mihotich
Printed in Latvia by Livonia Print

A proportion of this book has appeared online at
www.theschooloflife.com/thebookoflife

Every effort has been made to contact the copyright holders of
the material reproduced in this book. If any have been
inadvertently overlooked, the publisher will be pleased to make
restitution at the earliest opportunity.

The School of Life is a resource for helping us understand
ourselves, for improving our relationships, our careers and our
social lives – as well as for helping us find calm and get more
out of our leisure hours. We do this through creating films,
workshops, books and gifts.

www.theschooloflife.com

ISBN 978-0-9955736-2-8

10 9 8 7 6

Contents

I

Why You Will Marry
the Wrong Person

Anyone we might marry could, of course, be a little bit wrong for us. We don't expect bliss every day. We know that perfection is not on the cards. Nevertheless, there are couples who display such deep-seated incompatibility, such heightened rage and disappointment, that we have to conclude that something else is at play beyond the normal scratchiness: they appear to have married the wrong person.

How do such errors happen in our enlightened, knowledge-rich times? We can say straight off that they occur with appalling ease and regularity. Academic achievement and career success seem to provide no vaccines. Otherwise intelligent people daily and blithely make the move.

Given that it is about the single costliest mistake any of us can make (it places rather large burdens on the state, employers and the next generation too), there would seem to be few issues more important than that of marrying intelligently.

It's all the more poignant that the reasons why people make the wrong choices are rather easy to lay out and unsurprising in their structure. We ruin our lives for reasons that can be summed up in an essay. They tend to fall into some of the following basic categories.

A standard question on any early dinner date should be quite simply: 'And how are you mad?'

1
We don't understand ourselves

When first looking out for a partner, the requirements we come up with are coloured by a beautifully non-specific sentimental vagueness: we'll say we really want to find someone who is 'kind' or 'fun to be with', 'attractive' or 'up for adventure...'.

It isn't that such desires are wrong; they are just not remotely precise enough in their understanding of what we in particular are going to require in order to stand a chance of being happy – or, more accurately, not consistently glum.

All of us are crazy in very particular ways. We're distinctively neurotic, unbalanced and immature, but don't know quite the details because no one ever encourages us too hard to find them out. An urgent, primary task of any lover is therefore to get a handle on the specific ways in which they are mad. They have to get up to speed on their individual neuroses. They have to grasp where these have come from, what they make them do – and, most importantly, what sort of people either provoke or assuage them. A good partnership is not so much one between two healthy people (there aren't many of these on the planet), it's one between two demented people who have had the skill or luck to find a non-threatening accommodation between their relative insanities.

The feeling that we might not be too difficult to live with should set off alarm bells. The only people we can think of as normal are those we don't know very well. The question is just where the problems will lie: perhaps we have a latent tendency to get furious when someone disagrees with us, or we can only relax when we are working, or we're a bit tricky around intimacy after sex, or we've never been so good at explaining what's on our minds when we're worried. It's these sorts of issues that – over decades – create catastrophes and that we should ideally therefore need to know about way ahead of time, in order to look out for people who are optimally designed to withstand them. A standard question on any early dinner date should be quite simply: 'And how are you mad?'

The problem is that knowledge of our own neuroses is not at all easy to come by. It can take years and situations we have had no experience of. Prior to marriage, we're rarely involved in dynamics that properly hold up a mirror to our disturbances. Whenever more casual relationships threaten to reveal the 'difficult' side of our natures, we tend to blame the partner – and call it a day. As for our friends, they predictably don't care enough about us to have any motive to probe our real selves. They only want a nice evening out. Therefore, we end up blind to the awkward sides of our natures. On our own, when we're furious, we don't shout, as there's no one there to listen – and therefore we overlook the true, worrying strength of our capacity for fury. Or we work all the time without grasping, because there's no one calling us to come for dinner, how we manically use our jobs to gain a sense of control over life – and how we might cause hell if anyone tried to stop us labouring. At night, all we're aware of is how sweet it would be to cuddle with someone, but we have no opportunity to face up to the intimacy-avoiding side of us that would start to make us cold and strange if ever it felt we were too deeply committed to someone. One of the greatest privileges of being on one's own is the flattering illusion that one is, in truth, really quite an easy person to live with.

With such a poor level of understanding of our characters, no wonder we aren't in any position to know who we should be looking out for.

2
We don't understand
other people

This problem is compounded because other people are stuck at the same low level of self-knowledge as we are. However well-meaning they might be, they too are in no position to grasp, let alone inform us, of what is wrong with them.

Naturally, we make a stab at trying to know them. We go and visit their families, perhaps the place they first went to school. We look at photos; we meet their friends. All this contributes to a sense that we've done our homework. But it's like a novice pilot assuming they can fly after sending a paper plane successfully around the room.

In a wiser society, prospective partners would put each other through detailed psychological questionnaires and send themselves off to be assessed at length by teams of psychologists. By 2100, this will no longer sound like a joke. The mystery will be why it took humanity so long to get to this point.

We need to know the intimate functioning of the psyche

of the person we're planning to marry. We need to know their attitudes to, and stance on, authority, humiliation, introspection, sexual intimacy, money, children, ageing, fidelity and a hundred things besides. This knowledge won't be available via a standard chat. We need a level of insight currently generally only available to psychological professionals at the PhD level.

In the absence of this, we are led – in large part – by what they look like. It matters immensely, of course. We keep thinking how beautiful they look. There seems to be so much information to be gleaned from their eyes, nose, shape of forehead, distribution of freckles, smiles… . But this is about as wise as thinking that a photograph of the outside of a power station can tell us the essentials of nuclear fission.

We 'project' a range of perfections onto the beloved on the basis of only a little evidence. In elaborating a whole personality from a few small – but hugely evocative – details, we are doing for the inner character of a person what our eyes naturally do with the sketch of a face.

We don't see this picture (by Henri Matisse) as a depiction of someone who has no nostrils, eight strands of hair and no eyelashes. Without even noticing that we are doing it, we fill in the missing parts. Our brains are primed to take tiny visual hints and construct entire figures from them – and we do the same when it comes to the character of our prospective spouse. We are – much more than we give ourselves credit for, and to our great cost – inveterate artists of elaboration.

The level of knowledge we need for a marriage to work is higher than our society is prepared to countenance, recognise and accommodate – and our social practices do nothing to prevent us slipping off the precipice. We are collectively a great deal more interested in a beautiful wedding than a tolerable marriage.

Henri Matisse, *La Pompadour*, 1951

3
We aren't used to
being happy

We believe we seek happiness in love, but it's not quite that simple. What at times it seems we actually seek is *familiarity* – which may well complicate any plans we might have for happiness.

We recreate in adult relationships some of the feelings we knew in childhood. It was as children that we first came to know and understand what love meant. But unfortunately, the lessons we picked up may not have been straightforward. The love we knew as children may have come entwined with other, less pleasant dynamics: being controlled, feeling humiliated, being abandoned, never communicating – in short: suffering.

As adults, we may then reject certain healthy candidates whom we encounter, not because they are wrong, but precisely because they are too well-balanced (too mature, too understanding, too reliable), and this rightness feels unfamiliar and alien, almost oppressive. We head instead to candidates whom our unconscious is drawn to, not because they will please us, but because they will frustrate us in familiar ways.

We marry the wrong people because the right ones feel wrong – undeserved. We marry wrongly because we have no experience of health and because we don't – whatever we may say – ultimately associate being loved with feeling satisfied.

4
Being single
is so awful

One is never in a good frame of mind to choose a partner rationally when remaining single has come to feel unbearable. We have to be utterly at peace with the prospect of many years of solitude in order to have any chance of forming a good relationship. Or we'll love no longer being single rather more than we love the partner who spared us being so.

But unfortunately, after a certain age, society makes singlehood dangerously unpleasant. Communal life starts to wither; couples are too threatened by the independence of the single to invite them around very often; one starts to feel a leper when going to the cinema alone. Sex is hard to come by as well. For all the new gadgets and supposed freedoms of modernity, it continues to be maddeningly hard to get laid – and expecting to do so regularly with new people often ends in searing humiliation.

Far better to rearrange society so that it resembles a university or a kibbutz – with communal eating, shared facilities, constant parties and free sexual mingling... .

That way, anyone who did decide marriage was for them would be sure they were doing it for the positives of coupledom rather than as an escape from the negatives of singlehood.

When sex was only available within marriage, people recognised that this led people to marry for the wrong reasons: to obtain something that was artificially restricted in society as a whole. People are free to make much better choices about who they marry now they're not simply responding to a desperate desire for sex.

But we retain shortages in other areas. When company is only properly available in couples, people will pair up just to spare themselves loneliness. It's time to liberate 'companionship' from the shackles of coupledom and make it as widely and as easily available as sexual liberators wanted sex to be.

5
Instinct has too much prestige

Back in the olden days, marriage was a rational business, all to do with matching your bit of land with theirs. It was cold, ruthless and disconnected from the happiness of the protagonists. We are still traumatised by this.

What replaced the Marriage of Reason was the Marriage of Instinct, the Romantic marriage. It dictated that how one felt about someone should be the only guide to action. If one felt 'in love', that was enough. No more questions asked. Feeling was triumphant. Outsiders could only applaud the feeling's arrival, respecting it as one might the visitation of a divine spirit. Parents might be aghast, but they had to suppose that only a couple could ever really know what was good for themselves. We have for three hundred years been in collective reaction against many centuries of very unhelpful interference based on prejudice, snobbery and lack of imagination.

So pedantic and cautious was the old Marriage of Reason that one of the features of the Marriage of Feeling is the assumption that one shouldn't think too much about why one is marrying. To analyse the decision feels 'un-Romantic'. To write out charts of pros and cons seems absurd and cold. The most Romantic thing one can do is just to propose quickly and suddenly, perhaps after only a few weeks, in a rush of enthusiasm – without any chance to do the horrible 'reasoning' that guaranteed misery to people for thousands of years previously. The recklessness at play seems a sign that the marriage can work, precisely because the old kind of 'safety' was such a danger to one's happiness.

6
We don't go to
schools of love

The time has come for a third kind of marriage: the Marriage of Psychology, where one doesn't marry either just for practical reasons (land, money, etc.), or for intuitive reasons ('strong feelings'), but where our aspirations are properly submitted to examination and soberly understood, over many months, in the light of the daunting complexities of our respective psyches.

Presently, we marry without any information. We almost never read books specifically on the subject, we never spend more than a short time with children, and we don't rigorously interrogate other married couples or speak with any sincerity to divorced ones. We go into it without any insightful reasons as to why marriages fail – beyond what we presume to be the idiocy or lack of imagination of their protagonists.

In the long-gone age of the Marriage of Reason, we might have considered the following criteria when marrying:

- who are their parents?
- how much land do they have?
- how culturally similar are they?

In the Romantic age, we might have looked out for the following signs to determine rightness:

- an inability to stop thinking of the lover
- a sexual obsession
- a belief that they are an angel
- a longing for constant contact

For the age of the Marriage of Psychology, we need a new set of criteria. We should wonder:

- how are they mad?
- how can we raise children with them?
- how can we develop together?
- how can we remain friends?
- how can we on the accommodate our competing needs for extracurricular sex on the one hand and loyalty on the other?

7
We want to freeze happiness

We have a desperate and fateful urge to try to make nice things permanent. We want to own the car we saw on the screen; we want to live in the country we enjoyed as a tourist. And we want to marry the person we are having a terrific time with at the moment.

We imagine that marriage is a guarantor of the happiness we're presently enjoying with someone. It will make permanent what might otherwise be fleeting. It will help us to bottle our joy – the joy we felt when the thought of proposing first came to us: we were in Venice, on the lagoon, in a motorboat, with the evening sun throwing golden flakes of light across the sea, the prospect of dinner in a little fish restaurant, our beloved in a cashmere jumper in our arms... We got married to make this feeling permanent.

Unfortunately, there is no causal or necessary connection between marriage and this sort of feeling. The feeling was produced by Venice, a time of day, a lack of work, an excitement at dinner, a two-month acquaintance with someone... none of which 'marriage' increases or guarantees.

Marriage doesn't freeze the moment at all. That moment was dependent on the fact that you had only known each other for a bit, that you weren't working, that you were staying in a beautiful hotel near the Grand Canal, that you'd had a pleasant afternoon in the Guggenheim Museum, that you'd just had a chocolate gelato... .

Getting married has no power to keep a relationship at this beautiful stage. It is not in command of the ingredients of happiness that propelled us into it. In fact, marriage will decisively move the relationship to another, very different stage: to a suburban house, a long commute, two small children. The only ingredient in common is the partner. And that might have been the wrong ingredient to bottle.

The Impressionist painters of the nineteenth century had an implicit philosophy of transience that points us in a wise direction. They accepted the transience of happiness as an inherent feature of existence and they could in turn help us to grow more at peace with it. Alfred Sisley's painting of a winter scene in France focuses on a set of attractive but utterly fugitive things. Towards dusk, the

27

sun nearly breaks through the landscape. For a little time, the glow of the sky makes the bare branches less severe. The snow and the grey walls have a quiet harmony; the cold seems manageable, almost exciting. In a few minutes, night will close in.

Impressionism is interested in the fact that the things we love most change, are only around a very short time and then disappear. It celebrates the sort of happiness that lasts a few minutes, rather than years. In this painting, the snow looks lovely, but it will melt. The sky is beautiful at this moment, but it is about to go dark. This style of art cultivates a skill that extends far beyond art itself: a skill at accepting and attending to short-lived moments of satisfaction.

The peaks of life tend to be brief. Happiness doesn't come in year-long blocks. With the Impressionists to guide us, we should be ready to appreciate isolated moments of everyday paradise whenever they come our way, without making the mistake of thinking them permanent; without the need to turn them into a 'marriage'.

Alfred Sisley, *The Watering Place at Marly-le-Roi*, c.1875

8
We believe we
are special

The statistics are not encouraging. Everyone has before them plenty of examples of terrible marriages. They've seen their friends try it and come unstuck. They know perfectly well that – in general – marriages face immense challenges. And yet we do not easily apply this insight to our own case. Without specifically formulating it, we assume that misery is a rule that applies to other people.

That's because a raw statistical chance of one in two of failing at marriage seems wholly acceptable, given that – when we are in love – we feel we have already beaten far more extraordinary odds. The beloved feels like around one in a million. With such a winning streak, the gamble of marrying a person seems entirely containable.

We silently exclude ourselves from the general principle of marital unhappiness. We're not to be blamed for this. But we could benefit from being encouraged to see ourselves as invariably a little exposed to the general fate.

The peaks
of life tend to
be brief.
Happiness
doesn't come
in year-long
blocks.

9
We want to stop thinking about love

Before we get married, we are likely to have had many years of turbulence in our love lives. We will have tried to get together with people who didn't like us; we will have started and broken up unions; we will have gone out to a succession of parties, in the hope of meeting someone; and known excitement and searing disappointment.

No wonder if, at a certain point, we have had enough. Part of the reason we feel like getting married is to interrupt the all-consuming grip that love has over our psyches. We are exhausted by the melodramas and thrills that go nowhere. We are restless for other challenges. We hope that marriage can conclusively end love's painful rule over our lives.

Marriage can't and won't do this: there is as much doubt, hope, fear, rejection and betrayal inside a marriage as there is outside of one. It's only from the perspective of singledom that a marriage can look peaceful, uneventful – and enviably boring.

—

Preparing us for marriage is, ideally, an educational task that falls on culture as a whole. We have stopped believing in dynastic marriages. We are starting to see the drawbacks of Romantic marriages. Now comes the time for psychological marriages.

2

When is One Ready
to Get Married?

It used to be when you'd hit certain financial and social milestones: when you had a home to your name, a set of qualifications on the mantelpiece and a few cows and a parcel of land in your possession.

But when, under the influence of Romantic ideology, this grew to seem altogether too mercenary and calculating, the focus shifted to emotions. It came to be thought important to *feel* the right way. That was the true sign of a good union. And the right feelings included the sense that the other was 'the one', that you understood one another perfectly and that you'd both never want to sleep with anyone else again.

These ideas, though touching, have proved to be an almost sure recipe for the eventual dissolution of marriages – and have caused havoc in the emotional lives of millions of otherwise cautious and well-meaning couples.

As a corrective to them, what follows is a proposal for a very different set of principles, more Classical in temper, which indicate when two people should properly consider themselves ready for marriage.

We are ready for marriage...

1
When we give up
on perfection

We should not only admit in a general way that the person we are marrying is very far from perfect. We should also grasp the specifics of their imperfections: how they will be irritating, difficult, sometimes irrational, and often unable to sympathise with or understand us. Vows should be rewritten to include the terse line: 'I agree to marry this person even though they will, on a regular basis, drive me to distraction.'

However, these flaws should never be interpreted as merely capturing a local problem. No one else would be better. Everyone is as bad. We are a flawed species. Whomever one got together with would be radically imperfect in a host of deeply serious ways. One must conclusively kill the idea that things would be ideal with any other creature in this galaxy. There can only ever be a 'good-enough' marriage.

For this realisation to sink in, it helps to have had a number of relationships before marrying; not in order to have the chance to locate 'the right person', but so that one can have ample opportunity to discover at first hand, in many different contexts, the truth that everyone (even the most initially exciting prospect) really is a bit wrong from close up.

2
When we despair of
being understood

Love starts with the experience of being understood in a deeply and uncommonly supportive way. They understand the lonely parts of you; you don't have to explain why you find a particular joke so funny; you hate the same people; they too want to try out a particular sexual scenario.

This will not continue. Another vow should read: 'However much the other seems to understand me, there will always be large tracts of my psyche that will remain incomprehensible to them and anyone else.'

We shouldn't, therefore, blame our lovers for a dereliction of duty in failing to interpret and grasp our internal workings. They were not tragically inept. They simply couldn't understand who we were and what we needed – which is wholly normal. No one properly understands, and can therefore fully sympathise with, anyone else.

3
When we realise
we are crazy

This is deeply counter-intuitive. We seem so normal and mostly so good. It's the others who are the crazy ones.

But maturity is founded on an active sense of one's own folly. One is out of control for long periods; one has failed to master one's past; one projects unhelpfully; one is permanently anxious. One is, to put it mildly, an idiot.

If we are not regularly and very deeply embarrassed by who we are, it can only be because we haven't begun to understand our own narrative.

4
When we are ready to love rather than be loved

Confusingly, we speak of 'love' as one thing, rather than discerning the two very different varieties that lie beneath the single word: *being loved* and *loving*. We should marry when we are ready to do the latter and are aware of our unnatural, immature fixation on the former.

We start out knowing only about 'being loved'. It comes to seem – very wrongly – like the norm. To the child, it feels as if the parent is simply spontaneously on hand to comfort, guide, entertain, feed, clear up and remain almost always warm and cheerful. Parents don't reveal how often they have bitten their tongue, fought back the tears and been too tired to take off their clothes after a day of childcare. The relationship is almost entirely non-reciprocal. The parent loves, but they do not expect the favour to be returned in any significant way. The parent does not get upset when the child has not noticed the new haircut, asked carefully calibrated questions about how the meeting at work went or suggested that they go upstairs to take a nap. Parent and child may both 'love', but each party is on a very different end of the axis, unbeknownst to the child.

In adulthood, when we first say we long for love, what we predominantly mean is that we want to *be* loved as we were once loved by a parent. We want a recreation in adulthood of what it felt like to be ministered to and indulged. In a secret part of our minds, we picture someone who will understand our needs, bring us what we want, be immensely patient and sympathetic with us, act selflessly and make it all better.

This is – naturally – a disaster. For a marriage to work, we need to move firmly out of the child – and into the parental position. We need to become someone who will be willing to subordinate their own demands and concerns to the needs of another.

There's a further lesson to be learned. When a child says to its parent 'I hate you', the parent does not automatically go numb with shock or threaten to leave the house and never come back, because the parent knows that the child is not giving the executive summary of a deeply thought-out and patient investigation into the state of the relationship. The cause of these words might be hunger, a lost but crucial piece of Lego, the fact that they went to

43

a cocktail party last night, that they won't let them play a computer game, or that they have an earache... .

Parents become very good at not hearing the explicit words and listening instead to what the child means but doesn't yet know how to say: 'I'm lonely, in pain, or frightened' – distress that then unfairly comes out as an attack on the safest, kindest, most reliable thing in the child's world: the parent.

We find it exceptionally hard to make this move with our partners: to hear what they truly mean, rather than responding (furiously) to what they are saying.

A third vow should state: 'Whenever I have the strength in me to do so, I will imitate those who once loved me and take care of my partner as these figures cared for me. The task isn't an unfair chore or a departure from the true nature of love. It is the only kind of love really worthy of that exalted word.'

No one properly understands, and can therefore fully sympathise with, anyone else.

5
When we are ready
for administration

The Romantic person instinctively sees marriage in terms of emotions. But what a couple actually get up to together over a lifetime has much more in common with the workings of a small business. They must draw up work rosters, clean, chauffeur, cook, fix, throw away, hire, fire, reconcile and budget.

None of these activities have any glamour whatsoever within the current arrangement of society. Those obliged to do them are therefore highly likely to resent them and feel that something has gone wrong with their lives for having to involve themselves so closely with them. And yet these tasks are what is truly 'romantic' in the sense of 'conducive and sustaining of love'. They should be interpreted as the bedrock of a successful marriage and accorded all the honour currently given to other activities in society, like mountain climbing or motor sport.

A central vow should read: 'I accept the dignity of the ironing board.'

6
When we understand that sex and love do and don't belong together

The Romantic view expects that love and sex will be aligned. But in truth, they won't stay so beyond a few months or, at best, one or two years. This is not anyone's fault. Because marriage has other key concerns (companionship, administration, another generation), sex will suffer. We are ready to get married when we accept a large degree of sexual resignation and the task of sublimation.

Both parties must therefore scrupulously avoid making the marriage 'about sex'. They must also, from the outset, plan for the most challenging issue that will, statistically speaking, arise for them: that one or the other will have affairs. Someone is properly ready for marriage when they are ready to behave maturely around betraying and being betrayed.

The inexperienced, immature view of betrayal goes like this: sex doesn't have to be part of love. It can be quick and meaningless, just like playing tennis. Two people shouldn't try to own each other's bodies. It's just a bit of fun. So one's partner shouldn't mind so much.

But this is wilfully to ignore impregnable basics of human nature. No one can be the victim of adultery and not feel that they have been found fundamentally wanting and cut to the core of their being. They will never get over it. It makes no sense, of course, but that isn't the point. Many things about us make little sense – and yet have to be respected. The adulterer has to be ready to honour and forgive the partner's extreme capacity for jealousy, and so must, as far as is possible, resist the urge to have sex with other people, must take every possible measure to prevent it being known if they do, and must respond with extraordinary kindness and patience if the truth does ever emerge. They should above all never try to persuade their partner that it isn't right to be jealous or that jealousy is unnatural, 'bad' or a bourgeois construct.

On the other side of the equation, one should ready oneself for betrayal. That is, one should make strenuous efforts to try to understand what might go through the partner's mind when they have sex with someone else. One is likely to think that there is no other option but that they are deliberately trying to humiliate one and that all their love has evaporated. The more likely truth – that one's partner just wants to have more, or different, sex – is as hard to master as Mandarin or the oboe and requires as much practice.

One is ready to get married when two very difficult things are in place: one is ready to believe in one's partner's genuine capacity to separate love and sex. And at the same time, one is ready to believe in one's partner's stubborn inability to keep love and sex apart.

Two people have to be able to master both feats, because they may – over a lifetime – be called upon to demonstrate both capacities. This – rather than a vow never to have sex with another human again – should be the relevant test for getting married.

7
When we are happy
to be taught and
calm about teaching

We are ready for marriage when we accept that, in certain very significant areas, our partners will be wiser, more reasonable and more mature than we are. We should want to learn from them. We should bear having things pointed out to us. We should, at key points, see them as the teacher and ourselves as pupils. At the same time, we should be ready to take on the task of teaching them certain things and, like good teachers, not shout, lose our tempers or expect them simply to know. Marriage should be recognised as a process of mutual education.

8
When we realise we're not that compatible

The Romantic view of marriage stresses that the 'right' person means someone who shares our tastes, interests and general attitudes to life. This might be true in the short term. But, over an extended period of time, the relevance of this fades dramatically, because differences inevitably emerge. The person who is truly best suited to us is not the person who shares our tastes, but the person who can negotiate differences in taste intelligently and wisely.

Rather than some notional idea of perfect complementarity, it is the capacity to tolerate difference that is the true marker of the 'right' person. Compatibility is an achievement of love; it shouldn't be its precondition.

It is
the capacity
to tolerate
difference
that is
the true marker
of the 'right'
person.

Conclusion

We have accepted that it is a truly good idea to attend some classes before having children. This is now the norm for all educated people in all developed nations.

Yet there is as yet no widespread acceptability for the idea of taking classes before getting married. The results are around for all to see.

The time has come to bury the Romantic intuition-based view of marriage and to learn to practise and rehearse marriage as one would iceskating or violin playing, activities no more complex and no more deserving of systematic periods of instruction.

For now, while the infrastructure of new vows and classes is put in place, we all deserve untold sympathy for our struggles. We are trying to do something enormously difficult without the bare minimum of support necessary. It is not surprising if – very often – we don't succeed.

3

How Love Stories
Ruin Our Love Lives

It sounds strange to ask what a love story might be for. We tend not to wonder too much what role made-up stories should play in our lives. Generally, we suppose we just read them for 'entertainment'.

Yet that is to be unstrategic about a major cultural resource. A love novel is a machine for simulating experience, a 'life simulator' and – like its flight equivalent – it allows us safely to experience what it might – in real life – take us years and great danger to go through. Unaided, we are puny in our powers of empathy and comprehension, isolated from the inner lives of others, limited in our experiences, short of time and able to encounter only a tiny portion of the world first hand. Fiction extends our range – it takes us inside the intimate consciousness of strangers, and it lets us sit in on experiences that would be terrifying or reckless in reality; it lends us more lives than we have been given.

There are three ways in particular in which novels deliver their assistance:

1
As cautionary tales

Love stories give us early warnings. They alert us to dangers that we're not adept at recognising: where envy might lead us, what indifference can do to a relationship, where lust can drive us… . They trace the links between apparently minor errors of personality and the monumental catastrophes they can unleash, in the hope that by showing us the pitfalls, our own tendencies to disaster and folly may be curbed.

2
As maps of progress

Fiction provides models of development, demonstrations of triumph over difficulties, case studies in maturation and the acquisition of wisdom. We are carefully taken through ways in which certain people have learned, perhaps over many years and with much pain, how to cope with problems that are, in some ways, also our own.

3
As exhortations

There are many good things that we may not have known close up but that we would benefit from experiencing – and that fiction can create for us. It can show us a couple who have understood how to resolve their difficulties with grace and humour, a father who can be at once authoritative and kind, and a mother who has an unhelpful desire for perfection. It's not simply that we need to know there are such people at large. It's that by spending time in their company, the painful lessons of human nature have an opportunity to rub off on us a little.

Unfortunately, there are too many bad love novels out there – by which one means novels that do not give us a correct map of love, that leave us unprepared to deal adequately with the difficulties of being in a couple. In moments of acute distress in relationships, our grief is too often complicated by a sense that things have become, for us alone, unusually and perversely difficult. Not only are we suffering, but it seems that our suffering has no equivalent in the lives of other more or less sane people.

Our attitudes to our own love lives are in large part formed by the tradition of the Romantic novel (which nowadays is advanced not only in literary fiction but in film, music and advertising). The narrative arts of the Romantic novel have unwittingly constructed a devilish template of expectations of what relationships are supposed to be like – in the light of which our own love lives often look grievously and deeply unsatisfying. We break up or feel ourselves cursed in significant part because we are exposed to the wrong works of literature.

If this 'wrong' kind is to be termed Romantic, then the right kind – of which there are so few – might be deemed Classical. Here are some of the differences:

Fiction lends us more lives than we have been given.

The plot

Romantic novel: In the archetypal Romantic novel, the drama hinges entirely on how a couple get together: the 'love story' is no such thing; it is merely the account of how love begins. All sorts of obstacles are placed in the way of love's birth, and the interest lies in watching their steady overcoming: there might be misunderstandings, bad luck, prejudice, war, a rival, a fear of intimacy, or – most poignantly – shyness... . But in the end, after tribulations, the right people eventually get into couples. Love begins – and the typical story ends.

Classical novel: This wiser, less immediately seductive genre knows that the real problem isn't finding a partner: it is tolerating them, and being tolerated, over a long time. It knows that the start of relationships is not the high point that Romantic culture assumes; it is merely the first step with a far longer, more ambivalent and yet quietly more heroic journey – on which it directs its intelligence and scrutiny.

Work

Romantic novel: The characters may have jobs, but on the whole they have little impact on their psyches. Work goes on somewhere else. What one does for a living is not thought relevant to an understanding of love.

Classical novel: Here we see that work is in fact a huge part of life, with an overwhelming role in shaping our relationships. Whatever our emotional dispositions, it is the stress of work that ends up generating a sizeable share of the trouble that lovers will have with each other.

Children

Romantic novel: Children are incidental, sweet symbols of mutual love, or naughty in an endearing way. They rarely cry, take up little time and are generally wise, exhibiting a native, unschooled intelligence.

Classical novel: In a wiser sort of story we would see that relationships are fundamentally oriented towards the having and raising of children – and at the same time, that children place the couple under unbearable strains. They kill the passion that made them possible. Life moves from the sublime to the quotidian. There are toys in the living room, pieces of chicken under the table, and no time to talk. Everyone is always tired. This too is love.

Practicalities

Romantic novel: In this genre, we have only a hazy idea of who does the housework. It is not seen as relevant to a relationship. Domesticity is a corrupting force and people who care a lot about it are likely to be unhappy in their relationships. We are unlikely to learn a great deal concerning a couple's thinking on homework or television for the under fours.

Classical novel: Here, relationships are understood to be institutions, not just emotions. Part of their rationale is to enable two people to function as a joint economic unit for the education of the next generation. This is in no way banal. There are opportunities for genuine heroism. Especially around laundry.

Sex

Romantic novel: Sex and love are shown to belong together. The high point of love is intercourse. Adultery, in the Romantic view, is therefore fatal: if you were with the right person you could never be unfaithful.

Classical novel: It knows that long-term love may not set up the best preconditions for sex. The Classical attitude sees love and sex as distinct and at times divergent themes in life. And therefore sexual problems do not in themselves indicate that a relationship is, overall, a disaster... .

Compatibility

Romantic novel: The Romantic novel cares about the harmony (or lack of it) between the souls of the protagonists. It believes that the fundamental challenge of emotional life is to find someone who completely understands us and with whom there need never be any more secrets. It believes that love is finding your other half, your spiritual twin. Love is not about training or education; it is an instinct, a feeling – and is generally mysterious in its workings.

Classical novel: It accepts that no one ever fully understands anyone else; that there must be secrets, that there will be loneliness, that there must be compromise. It believes that we have to learn how to sustain good relationships, that there are learnable skills involved, and that love is not just a chance endowment of nature.

–

The Romantic novel is deeply unhelpful. We have learned to judge ourselves by the hopes and expectations fostered by a misleading medium. By its standards, our own relationships are almost all damaged and unsatisfactory. No wonder separation or divorce so often appear to be inevitable.

They shouldn't be; we merely need to change our reading matter: to tell ourselves more accurate stories about the progress of relationships, stories that normalise troubles and show us an intelligent, helpful path through them.

The School of Life is a global organisation helping people lead more fulfilled lives. It is a resource for helping us understand ourselves, for improving our relationships, our careers and our social lives – as well as for helping us find calm and get more out of our leisure hours. We do this through films, workshops, books, gifts and community. You can find us online, in stores and in welcoming spaces around the globe.